Stick Insects and Ants

By Kevin Cunningham

21st Century Junior Library

Published in the United States of America by
Cherry Lake Publishing
Ann Arbor, Michigan
www.cherrylakepublishing.com

Content Adviser: Stephen Ditchkoff, Professor of Wildlife Ecology and Management, Auburn University, Alabama
Reading Adviser: Marla Conn MS, Ed., Literacy specialist, Read-Ability, Inc.

Photo Credits: © Kevin Wells Photography/Shutterstock, cover, 1, 20; © Anterovium/istock, 4; © Goddard_Photography/Thinkstock, 6; © David W. Leindecker/Shutterstock, 8; © imageBROKER / Alamy Stock Photo, 10; © Meisterphotos | Dreamstime.com - Black Social Ant Colony Close Up Photo, 12; © Imaake/Shutterstock, 14; © AG-PHOTOS/Shutterstock, 16; © Stefan Sollfors / Alamy Stock Photo, 18

Library of Congress Cataloging-in-Publication Data

Names: Cunningham, Kevin, 1966- author.
Title: Stick insects and ants / Kevin Cunningham.
Description: Ann Arbor, MI : Cherry Lake Publishing, 2016. | Series: Better together | Audience: K to grade 3. | Includes bibliographical references and index.
Identifiers: LCCN 2015049541 | ISBN 9781634710879 (hardcover) | ISBN 9781634712859 (pbk.) | ISBN 9781634711869 (pdf) | ISBN 9781634713849 (ebook)
Subjects: LCSH: Mutualism (Biology)–Juvenile literature. | Ants–Juvenile literature. | Stick insects–Juvenile literature. | Animal behavior–Juvenile literature.
Classification: LCC QH548.3 .C8675 2016 | DDC 591.7/85–dc23
LC record available at http://lccn.loc.gov/2015049541

Cherry Lake Publishing would like to acknowledge the work of The Partnership for 21st Century Skills.
Please visit *www.p21.org* for more information.

Printed in the United States of America
Corporate Graphics

CONTENTS

There are more than 12,000 species of ants in the world.

Egg Hunt

A group of ants marches into the forest. The queen of the ant **colony** waits for the group to return with food.

One ant finds eggs on the ground. It tells the others that it sees food. The ants hurry forward. One by one, every ant grabs an egg to take home.

The eggs are part of a **partnership** the ants have with another insect. Their partner is a stick insect.

Stick insects look just like moving sticks.
They are often called walking sticks.

Stick Tricks

Stick insects are masters of **disguise**. Humans, birds, and frogs can look right at a stick insect and never see it. That's because it looks like a stick. It has a green, brown, or gray body. It blends in with plants.

Stick insects come in many sizes. Some barely manage to grow to 0.5 inches (1.3 centimeters) long. Others get much

Stick insects might look like cool pets, but they should stay in nature.

bigger. The giant walking stick stretches to 7 inches (17.8 cm). It is the longest insect in the United States.

Birds, lizards, frogs, and other insects eat the stick insect. Its disguise doesn't always work. A stick insect must also **defend** itself to survive. Stick insects can do this by acting dead. They look even more like sticks. Some kinds of stick insects let a hunter tear off their leg. The stick insects keep running away.

Stick insects **reproduce** by laying eggs. The eggs are tiny and shaped like beans. Females drop them from high up

Stick insect larvae look like a smaller version of an adult stick insect.

in trees. The eggs cannot stay on the forest floor. Other animals might eat them all. Then there would be no more stick insects.

But stick insects get help from ants. They have an important partnership.

Think!

One type of stick insect shoots out a fluid to defend itself. The fluid smells awful! Can you think of other animals that use bad smells to scare off enemies?

Ant colonies can be enormous. The largest true colony ever found was 500 square feet (46 square meters).

Hard Workers

Ants work together. They live in large groups. Scientists call them **social** insects. Some kinds of ants make homes in piles of dirt. Others prefer trees. Many ants dig out a colony under the ground.

The colony contains many rooms. A queen is very important to the colony. Only the queen reproduces. All the ants hatch from her eggs. She is every ant's mother.

Ants are omnivores. They eat meat and plants.

Many of the ant **larvae** grow into **worker ants**. Worker ants are always female. They have incredible strength. A worker can carry three times its own weight. That's like you carrying over 250 pounds (113.4 kilograms).

Look!

Watch for ants the next time you take a walk. The ants you see will be workers. What work are they doing? Do you see ants in groups? Or do you see single ants exploring on their own?

An ant colony consists of the queen, female worker ants, and male ants.

Worker ants go out into the world. They find what a colony needs. That includes food. Many types of ants eat insect eggs. That includes eggs from stick insects.

The eggs are heavy. But the workers use their strength. They carry the eggs back to the colony.

Ask Questions!

Ants live almost everywhere on earth. Why do you think they do well in so many places? Could working together make a difference? Do other social animals work as a group to make their lives better? Ask a parent, teacher, or librarian for help finding the answer.

Stick insect eggs have no defenses of their own.

Hiding Place

How do stick insects survive if ants eat their eggs? Ants only eat part of the egg.

A hungry ant visits a food storage room. There it finds food brought in by the workers. Stick insect eggs have a **knob** on top. The knob is full of fat. The ant eats the knob, but it ignores the rest of the egg and tosses it into a garbage room. The eggs sit

Stick insects and ants live all over the world.
They help each other all over the world.

safely with the trash. No ants want them. No other animals can get to them.

The stick insect larvae, called **nymphs**, often hatch in spring. The tiny nymphs dig or crawl out of the ant colony. Once outside, they eat. They grow. They become adult stick insects.

Soon the adult females drop new eggs. Then the worker ants march out to grab the eggs. One of nature's awesome partnerships lives on!

GLOSSARY

colony (KAH-luh-nee) a large group of animals that live together

defend (di-FEND) do something to escape an attack

disguise (dis-GIZE) a way of changing appearance to stay safe

knob (NOB) a lump at the end of something

larvae (LAHR-vee) baby ants or insects

nymphs (NIMFS) the name for baby stick insects

partnership (PAHRT-nur-ship) two animals working together

reproduce (ree-pruh-DOOS) to have babies

social (SO-shul) living in large groups

worker ants (WERK-er ANTS) ants that find food and do other work for the colony

FIND OUT MORE

BOOKS

Bestor, Sheri M., with Jonny Lambert (illustrator). *Good Trick, Walking Stick!* Ann Arbor, MI: Sleeping Bear, 2016.

Bodden, Valerie. *Ants*. Mankato, MN: Creative Education, 2013.

Gray, Leon. *Walking Sticks: The World's Longest Insects*. New York: Bearport, 2013.

Micucci, Charles. *The Life and Times of an Ant*. Boston: Houghton Mifflin Company, 2003.

WEB SITES

Ants—Attenborough: Life in the Undergrowth—BBC
www.youtube.com/watch?v=Er-OnJCn1gg

National Geographic—Ant
http://animals.nationalgeographic.com/animals/bugs/ant

San Diego Zoo—Stick Insect
http://animals.sandiegozoo.org/animals/stick-insect

Zoos Victoria—Lord Howe Island Stick Insect
https://vimeo.com/14413689

INDEX

ABOUT THE AUTHOR

Kevin Cunningham is the author of more than 60 books. He lives near Chicago.